D1485529

The
A–Z
of
Mindfulness

THE A–Z OF MINDFULNESS

An Hachette UK Company
www.hachette.co.uk

Summersdale Publishers Ltd
Part of Octopus Publishing Group Limited
Carmelite House
50 Victoria Embankment
LONDON
EC4Y 0DZ
UK

www.summersdale.com

Printed and bound in China

ISBN: 978-1-78783-273-2

Substantial discounts on bulk quantities of Summersdale books are available to corporations, professional associations and other organizations. For details contact general enquiries: telephone: +44 (0) 1243 771107 or email: enquiries@summersdale.com.

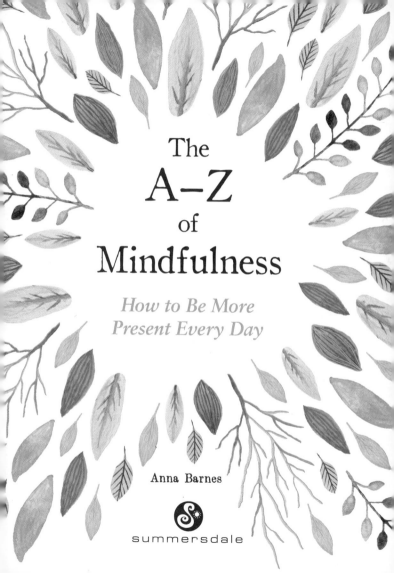

The
A–Z
of
Mindfulness

*How to Be More
Present Every Day*

Anna Barnes

summersdale

Introduction

What is mindfulness? Also known as present moment awareness, mindfulness is about focusing on the here and now, and letting go of thoughts and judgements.

Our busy modern lives are crammed full of things demanding our attention: to-do lists, replies to send, forms to fill in, bills to pay, deadlines to meet, people to see, mouths to feed. So it's easy to feel overwhelmed and forget to look after ourselves. Mindfulness is about bringing ourselves back from ruminating about the future or worries that consume our energy to experience the present moment fully, without conscious analysis.

Babies and very young children are experts at mindfulness. For them, everything is a source of wonder and fascination – things as ordinary as a cup or a chair, a scarf or a banana. With regular mindfulness practice, you can reawaken that inner child and that innate wonder. Pause and notice what your senses are sensing – what you smell, hear, see, taste and feel. The

simple act of focusing your awareness on one or more of your senses can be amazingly powerful, helping you feel grounded, calm and present in your life.

Mindfulness has helped millions of people the world over achieve balance, purpose and joy in their lives. This book is here to help you use it to improve your own life.

is for
Acceptance

Central to mindfulness practice is accepting our continuous stream of thoughts but, crucially, allowing our thoughts to disperse quietly in order to focus fully on the present moment. A never-ending series of thoughts can be exhausting, never allowing your mind to rest. In mindfulness, we allow ourselves to become aware of these thoughts, then simply let them go, like observing a cloud passing overhead.

Whenever a thought comes into your mind, no matter whether it's critical or positive, see it for what it is: a passing thought. Don't mistake it for substance. Thoughts are not reality; thoughts are not things. Accept them and let them pass.

Often, thoughts can be self-critical or destructive. Don't fight them; negative thoughts love to engage in combat, and they like to win. Just observe them, then bring your focus back to the present moment.

It can be enormously liberating when you first get the hang of this. You don't have to be ruled by your thoughts; you don't have to give them your attention. You can simply let them go.

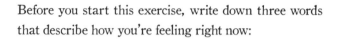

Before you start this exercise, write down three words that describe how you're feeling right now:

Passing clouds exercise

1. Begin by sitting or lying in a comfortable position. Focus on slowing your breathing.

2. Bring your awareness to any thoughts that surface. Simply acknowledge them without appraisal. Picture them as soft clouds, passing overhead on a gentle breeze. Let them pass and drift away.

3. Now bring your focus back to your breath.

This exercise can be repeated any time you feel anxious. It can help you to step back from your anxiety and restore a real sense of calm.

Now that you've completed the exercise, write down three words that describe how you're feeling:

Learn to accept and love yourself

as a flawed and imperfect

human... Accept your strengths

as well as your weaknesses.

David D. Burns

I am fully

present in

this moment.

B

is for
Breathing

It's something so automatic that we tend to take it for granted, yet how we breathe can have a profound effect on our well-being. Yoga and meditation practitioners talk about the quality of our breath. And since we each take in around 16 breaths a minute or 23,000 breaths a day – that's 680 million breaths in the average lifetime – you can see why quality is important. When we inhale, our lungs fill with air and oxygen is absorbed into our bloodstream. Our hearts pump oxygenated blood round our bodies, delivering essential oxygen to every cell.

Many people's unconscious breathing patterns are shallow and erratic, with shorter exhalations than inhalations. Extending our out-breath promotes relaxation. As you breathe out, let go. Allow your shoulders to drop and release tension with every exhale. Don't worry or berate yourself if your breaths are shallow and fast. With practice and patience you will be able to slow your breathing.

When we allow our breath to deepen, our tummies rise on the in-breath and our out-breath lengthens. This is called diaphragmatic breathing, which simply means that instead of pushing your chest out so that your lungs fill, you allow your diaphragm – the muscular band between your thorax and abdomen – to shift downward. This gives your body the nurturing and restorative benefit of each full breath. Mastering diaphragmatic breathing can increase your energy levels and concentration, while relaxing your muscles and calming your mind.

1. Find a comfortable position and listen to your breathing. How would you describe it? Are your in-breaths longer than your out-breaths? Notice the air passing through your nostrils and filling your lungs.

2. Now focus on slowing your breathing. In particular, slow your out-breath. Let your belly soften. Close your eyes and allow your breath to deepen. If your mind wanders, gently bring your focus back to the breath. Continue this for as long as you like.

3. Has your breathing slowed? Do you feel more centred? Note any observations here.

*I am open
to surprise.
Every cell in my
being is bursting
with life.*

is for
Colouring

Many people find colouring in to be relaxing. It's a great mindfulness activity because it allows you to focus all your attention on the page in front of you, on the movement of your pen or pencil, on filling in tiny shapes and gradually building that up. Experiment with leaving some areas blank instead of filling in every shape. Sometimes the white spaces can provide a satisfying aesthetic of their own.

Choose the pens or pencils you wish to use. How do they feel in your hand? You may wish to invest in a pack of quality pencils or fine-liner pens. Which colours are you drawn to today? Notice if you have picked muted or bright shades, or perhaps you prefer clashing colours. Don't try to assess the image while you colour; simply let your mind and body become fully absorbed in this activity.

Notice the texture of the paper against your fingertips, the sound of the pencil or pen against the paper, the smell of wax, wood pulp or ink. If your mind wanders, gently bring it back to the page. If you find you are hunching your shoulders or clenching your jaw, bring your awareness to these areas for a moment and let them relax.

Note how you feel afterward. Has your mind calmed into a more peaceful state?

Colour in the mandala

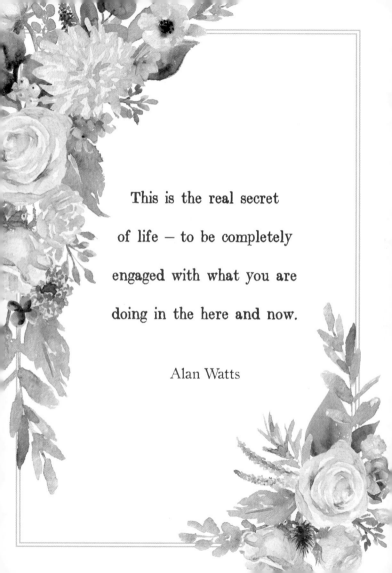

This is the real secret
of life — to be completely
engaged with what you are
doing in the here and now.

Alan Watts

D

is for
Daily

If you want mindfulness to have maximum impact, make it a regular aspect of your life. It could be a particular ritual that you choose to perform mindfully each day or it could be about taking responsibility for your time and well-being. Daily routines can become exhausting and monotonous, yet nurturing daily rituals can be revitalizing. What once was a chore can become something engaging.

First thing in the morning is a great time to practise mindfulness. Some people like to begin each day with a simple stretching or yoga sequence, while others like to perform a brief breathing meditation. Find something that works for you. One person may choose to write a stream-of-consciousness entry in their journal; another may prefer to have a mindful walk round their garden or neighbourhood, noticing details such as the chatter of birds, a gust of wind, a beeping horn, the quality of the light or a particular smell. Or you could repeat an affirmation out loud, such as, "This is a new day, and I am thankful for it," or "I'm going to pay attention and live every moment of this day."

You can bring mindfulness into many different aspects of your everyday life. Whether it's preparing a meal, sitting on a train or taking out the rubbish, you can choose to pay attention and complete simple tasks in a mindful way. Even automatic activities such as brushing your teeth, washing the dishes or driving can be undertaken in this way.

Sketch or jot down a daily activity or sequence of activities that you can perform mindfully. This could be a simple line drawing, cartoon or comic strip, or just a few keywords or phrases.

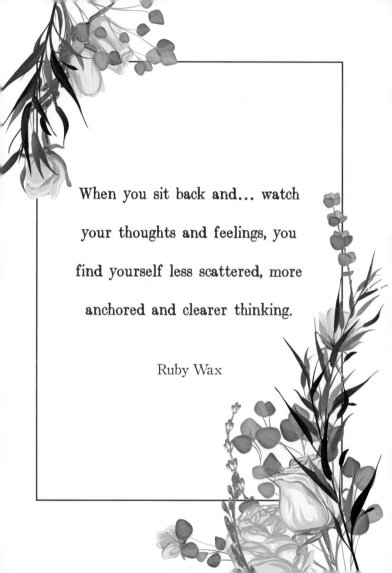

When you sit back and... watch your thoughts and feelings, you find yourself less scattered, more anchored and clearer thinking.

Ruby Wax

E

is for
Energy

In our busy world, with so many demands on our time, it's easy to become depleted of energy. Mindfulness enables you to still your mind and find clarity and calm, and it can work wonders for your energy levels. Do you ever feel you're just getting through the days without any real purpose and life is passing you by? If this rings true, then regular mindful practice can help restore your energy reserves and reawaken your innate ability to feel present and really live each day.

When our energy is low, even the little things that are normally manageable can become exhausting. Decision-making can feel stressful and draining. When we pause and accept the present moment, however, and allow ourselves to let go of all the "white noise" cluttering our minds, we restore our inner calm, a little like rebooting a computer.

It is also important to simplify your life. Unsubscribe from things you don't want. Stick to a handful of energizing activities that give you a sense of joy, peace or purpose. If your diary is too full, prune back the less important items until it feels like a good balance.

Anyone familiar with the Yerkes–Dodson law, which measures "performance" in relation to "arousal", will know that some mental arousal or stress is positive, to stimulate our bodies and minds. It is only when it exceeds the optimum level that it begins to rise into anxiety, hyperarousal and impaired performance. Mindfulness can help you find that perfect balance between too little and too much stimulation.

Food meditation

Take a piece of food that fits in the palm of your hand – a blueberry, perhaps, or a square of toast.

Consciously focus your attention on the item. How does it feel resting in your palm? How does it feel between your thumb and finger? Can you roll it around, or run your finger across the surface? Observe the texture. Is it soft or hard, rough or smooth, warm or cool? Be aware that you are experiencing it through your senses. How does it smell? Does the smell conjure up anything else for you? Examine your food item close up. Do you notice anything about it, about its shape or colour? Take a nibble. How do you experience the tastes and textures on your tongue? What flavours do you detect? Have another look now that you've bitten into it. Note the smells, how you're seeing it and the consistency. Is it changing while in contact with your skin?

Did you notice anything new, that you've never noticed before? Was there anything surprising about the experience?

I noticed…

I am capable,
I am calm.

Stepping out of the busyness... is perhaps the most beautiful offering we can make to our spirit.

Tara Brach

is for
Freedom

We all carry around with us our own personal history. For many people, this can mutate into the weight of past regrets and mistakes, carrying that baggage into the present. Unless we learn to let go, this can become a burden. Mindfulness practice frees you up to release those memories and liberate yourself from self-limiting beliefs. Realize that even your impression or memory of something may not be based on an objective reality – it is your subjective interpretation.

Forgive yourself any past regrets and make a conscious decision to let them go and move on. If a weight presses down on you from the past or a mental fog clouds your thought processes and decision-making, let it lift like a mist dissipating. Try to bring this sense of freedom into your thought processes. Focus on freeing up your mental outlook and developing a growth mindset, instead of engaging in the unhelpful habit of making qualitative judgements. When you meet a new person or try something new, instead of making automatic assumptions, keep an open mind. Bring this freedom into your body, too; practise moving in a freer way, rather than tensing up muscle groups that aren't required for a particular movement.

Developing a regular mindfulness practice can help you to achieve an inner and outer freedom, focusing your attention and teaching you to appreciate the world around you. If you find you are locked in behavioural patterns that are rooted in habit, understand you are free to let go of those patterns and practise new, more nurturing choices.

Colour in the mandala

Do not dwell in the past,

do not dream of the future,

concentrate the mind on

the present moment.

Buddhist proverb

is for
Gardening

If you are a gardener, you will already know how mindful an activity gardening can be. But you don't have to be green-fingered or have your own garden or allotment in order to enjoy the benefits. If you don't have your own outdoor space, you can still plant a window box or grow herbs and vegetables as well as houseplants. If you have a balcony or shared front door, you can plant up pots with flowers to provide year-round colour.

Planting and gardening are wonderfully therapeutic. The acts of handling soil, sowing seeds, planting seedlings, observing them as they germinate, and caring for another living thing and watching it grow are immensely absorbing and grounding. Planting something you can eat can be especially rewarding.

Grow-your-own kits can be particularly fun for adults and children alike. Options include herbs and spices, such as basil and coriander, chillies, succulents and cacti.

Sprouting broad beans or other beans in a jar and watching the roots and shoots emerge and then grow can also be a great introduction to mindful gardening. To try this, stuff a large, clean jar with a dampened paper towel. Place your broad bean halfway down, so you can see it from the outside of the jar. You could place one to three beans around the edge. Place your jar in a warm, dark place, keep the paper towels moist and check it daily.

Draw your own imaginary tree

Add roots and new growth daily. Add leaves, buds or fruits. Keep developing your tree until it is fully grown, or has outgrown this page!

Your heart is full
of fertile seeds,
waiting to sprout.

Morihei Ueshiba

is for
Health

Research studies consistently demonstrate a positive relationship between mindfulness and psychological health. Such is its proven beneficial reach that mindfulness is recognized by many national and international health bodies and is prescribed for a range of issues, including weight management, depression and anxiety, and pre- and post-natal health. Mindfulness practice is also used as a therapy for people with psychiatric disorders and children with additional needs, and by athletes to enhance performance. Mindfulness-based interventions have been shown to reduce both rumination and worry significantly, and regular practice is used as an effective preventative therapy to avert an array of mental health conditions.

Meanwhile, consuming nutritious foods and plenty of water, keeping alcohol and sugar consumption to a minimum and maintaining a healthy lifestyle, with regular exercise and sufficient sleep, will also help with energy levels and overall well-being.

Try creating and using your own health inventory. Look at your average week. What habits or activities do you engage in that are beneficial or damaging to your health? Remember to consider your mental as well as your physical health. Are there any unhelpful habits that you'd like to reduce or cut? Is there anything nurturing that you'd like to introduce? How would you like your health inventory to look in a year's time? What adjustments can you make, large or small?

Master the art of the breath and your body will shine with the radiance of a star.

Yoga Sutra

is for
Imagination

Curiosity is at the heart of mindfulness. Keeping our minds creative and open is a wonderful gift for our psyches and souls. Now is the time to let go of any self-limiting beliefs, such as "I'm terrible at X" or "I can't Y." Many of these beliefs – whether you think you can't draw, or you feel you can follow instructions but can't design things – are rooted in childhood. Somewhere along our journey we believe a negative statement about ourselves and allow it to take up permanent residence.

Yet every human brain is intrinsically inventive, and imagination is a wonder that continues to grow, as long as we remain open to its unlimited possibilities. Taking the time to appreciate the small details in the world and free your mind to wander can be great for decluttering your mind.

Creative activities are particularly good for mindfulness since they are extremely engrossing. Watch anybody engaged in a craft and it is clear the activity is absorbing all their focus. It's never too late to try a new creative pursuit. It doesn't have to be art; it could be cooking, gardening, playing a musical instrument, learning a language, woodwork, jewellery making, sport or photography.

Learning any new skill is incredibly mindful, as it absorbs all your attention. If you could take up a new interest, what would it be? Are there any clubs or evening classes you could sign up for to turn this from an idea into reality? Invest some time in your interests.

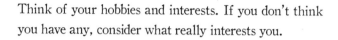

Think of your hobbies and interests. If you don't think you have any, consider what really interests you.

Note down some ideas here, then circle the ones that most appeal to you:

Seize the

day, savour

the moment.

is for
Joy

Let joy be part of the process, not the goal; when we seek happiness, we often can't find it. The secret is to focus on the small things. When we are absorbed in the present, that's when, in a moment of stillness, joy creeps in unnoticed.

One of the most effective ways of inviting joy into our lives is to unearth our natural playfulness. It's hardly surprising that many adults have forgotten how to play.

In our goal-driven culture, school and work can often be about targets, exams and achievements. However, a goal-oriented approach carried over into our social and personal lives can crush playfulness.

Play is a freely chosen behaviour that is unforced, uninhibited and unselfconscious. It is often spontaneous and is not reward-oriented, and while we associate it with children, adults can exhibit playful behaviour, too. It's simply being free to create and become absorbed in games and activities on your own or with others.

Another way to allow joy in is to engage socially. Social connections and networks can act as magical safety nets to buoy us up when needed, while joining in gives us the satisfaction of being part of something.

Social, psychological and work pressures, which can make us feel overwhelmed by everything we have to do, can inhibit our ability to experience joy. Physical clutter can also feel stressful. Decluttering your home and mind – simplifying both your outer and inner worlds – can help enormously, while appreciating the small details can bring the bigger picture to life.

Things that give me joy...

1. ....
....
....

2. ....
....
....

3. ....
....
....

The little things?
The little moments?
They aren't little.

Jon Kabat-Zinn

K

is for
Kindness

Mindfulness is about engaging more fully with the world. Sharing that enlightenment is a gift that benefits both the recipient and the giver, and research shows that feeling positive is good for heart health.

Cultivating empathy and compassion, for yourself as well as for others, is intrinsic to a more mindful existence. Kindness is a self-perpetuating win-win. When we experience kindness from others, we're more inclined to be kind ourselves. Both giver and benefactor feel good. Even if you feel anxious or drained, doing a simple kind deed for a friend, relative, neighbour or even a stranger can set in motion a snowball effect. The more we exercise kindness, the more natural it becomes. Sometimes the smallest of gestures can have the most impact, giving hope and comfort to someone in need.

Plan something kind to do for someone or something you care about. Follow it through. Extend that spirit of kindness, compassion and patience to yourself, too. Don't set unrealistic expectations of yourself or others; practise being generous and reasonable. The more you do it, the more it will become embedded in your behaviour.

*Write a list of self-care treats
that you can do to show
kindness to yourself*

1. ....
....
....

2. ....
....
....

3. ....
....
....

I am the driver of
my own destiny.

is for
Listening

Listen. What can you hear right now? The rustle of the paper of this book between your fingers? Noises in your house? Sounds outside?

By listening carefully we tune in to our sense of hearing, instead of relying solely on our dominant sense of sight. Focusing on hearing, or another of the senses, is a fundamental element of many mindfulness and meditation practices. You can focus on one at a time, in sequence or collectively.

Try training your attention on music, on a guitar strumming, distant birdsong, a breeze, the rhythmic churn of a washing machine, the changing of gears, your own voice singing or even silence, which may give way to an awareness of the sound of the pulse inside your head. If you are listening to music, choose either something very familiar or something that you wouldn't normally listen to. Zone in on a particular instrument or voice, and try to follow its line. Listen again and focus on a different instrument. Does the music create any images for you?

You can also practise listening to your inner self. Life can become cluttered at times, and we can get bogged down in excessive "noise". Learn to differentiate between the things you have the power to do something about and the things you don't. Liberate yourself from carrying other people's burdens in addition to your own. Listen to your own need for a simpler, more fulfilling life, then you'll have the energy and clarity of mind to support others.

What I hear...

How I feel...

What I can smell...

What textures surround me...

Breathe in every

detail of this moment.

If you want to conquer the anxiety of life, live in the moment, live in the breath.

Amit Ray

is for
Meditation

Many people find meditating helps them achieve a calm and enlightened state of mind, giving them the focus to go about their daily lives with greater energy and purpose.

One simple but effective meditation is the body scan. Begin by finding a comfortable position, close your eyes and focus on your breath, then scan your body mindfully. Starting with your toes, then the soles and tops of your feet, your ankles, calves, shins and knees, focus on each part of your body in turn, working your way up. Pay attention to each area for a few moments and observe any sensations you are experiencing. Notice if you are tensing any muscles – common areas of tension include the shoulders, jaw, forehead, forearms, buttocks, fingers and toes. Continue to breathe mindfully and release tension on an out-breath.

Another meditation you could try is the traffic light meditation. Next time you're stuck at a red light, pause. Instead of feeling frustration or worrying about being late, see the moment as a gift: a moment of stillness. Relax into your car seat. Become aware of your breath. Allow your shoulders to drop and your jaw to relax. Notice the sounds, the smells, the weather. When the light turns green, consider where you are going, not just in the literal sense. Proceed with your journey feeling calm and grounded.

Sometimes a brief moment of stillness is all we need to achieve clarity. You can do a similar meditation on a bus or train, in an elevator or while brushing your teeth, showering, cooking or queuing.

Colour in the mandala

The most precious gift we can offer

anyone is our attention. When

mindfulness embraces those we love,

they will bloom like flowers.

Thích Nhất Hạnh

N

is for
Nature

Taking advantage of the natural beauty around us is a wonderful way to cultivate greater mindfulness. The good news is that spending just two hours a week in nature has been linked to better health and well-being.

Physical and mental health benefits include a drop in cortisol levels and stress, encourages healthy blood pressure, an increase in oxygen and vitamin D, improved muscle tone, bone density and posture, and a boost to serotonin. Spending time in green spaces also has proven antibacterial, anti-inflammatory and immune-boosting effects, helps to maintain heart and brain health, reduces the risk of various diseases and increases longevity.

In our sometimes sterile modern world, it is easy to lose our connection with nature, especially if we live in an urban setting. Wild environments are naturally stimulating and reconnecting with the wilderness can help people experience sensory sharpening, a meditative state of mind and greater empowerment and purpose.

Engage your senses and stay open to what's happening around and within you. Look down at the living world at your feet. Kneel, sit or squat on the ground and take time to observe all the tiny details. It can be quite humbling to notice something new when you have been coming to a particular place for years. Now look up, and take in the world above you. Allow yourself to absorb the wonders of nature through all your senses.

Find a leaf. Feel it between your fingers.
Notice the texture. Observe the leaf's
shape, design, colour and temperature.
Study its unique pattern of veins. Breathe
in its smell. Do not assess or think
about the leaf; simply observe it.

Then let it blow away
in the breeze. If you
like, sit down and sketch
it from memory.

This will bring you back into the present moment. You can repeat this activity with a bud, a blade of grass, a coin, a paperclip or anything you find in your house, pocket or bag. Notice whether you find it more effective with natural or man-made items.

I can pause,

be still and

feel alive.

I only went out for a walk and finally concluded to stay out till sundown, for going out, I found, was really going in.

John Muir

is for
Ownership

Mindfulness requires commitment to yourself. Who says you have to be contactable 24/7? Who says you can't log out of social media or switch your phone to flight mode for a while?

If you want to live a fulfilled life, you need to take ownership of your time and show it the respect it deserves – the respect *you* deserve. Imagine you are letting out your time, like a holiday let. Set your own boundaries. It's wonderful to give time to others, but you also need to keep some aside just for you. It's not selfish; it's essential for your own health and well-being. It's like keeping your battery charged. If you don't set aside regular time for *you*, you run the risk of running your battery flat. How many times have you heard the expression "burnout"? It's what happens when we don't devote time to our own well-being.

Decide how much time you need to yourself to achieve that wellness. Ring-fence that time. It is your duty to look after yourself as well as everyone else in your life. A short window of protected time that is absolutely yours – even just ten minutes a day – can do wonders for your sense of joy. Listen to your needs. Listen to those aches and pains. If you're nursing a headache or a sore back, your body's trying to tell you to devote some time to yourself.

So claim back some time and protect it. Keep it safe. It's precious, and it's yours.

Things that make me
feel in control...

1. ....
   ....
   ....

2. ....
   ....
   ....

3. ....
   ....
   ....

I can't change the direction of the

wind, but I can adjust my sails.

Jimmy Dean

is for
Priorities

What is most important to you in your life? This is a fundamental question that we don't ask ourselves enough.

If you want a fulfilling life, it is essential to identify what really matters to you. Consider your average week. What duties and activities add something to your life? Can you spend more time on the things you enjoy? Conversely, sometimes the simplest of tasks can seem like insurmountable summits. What things leave you feeling stressed or worn out? Can you delegate some of them, or cut them out of your life completely? If that's not possible, can you learn to accept them without activating your stress response, and adopt a mindful attitude toward them? Sometimes approaching things from a different mindset can make a startling difference: something we perceived as stressful or challenging can come into focus as a straightforward task that we realize is well within our capability. Have the courage to sit up and begin to make adjustments.

By committing to yourself on this level, you will then have the energy to commit to the people who matter to you. Think of the people in your life. Who makes you feel good about yourself? Who makes you smile when you think about them? Who do you always look forward to seeing? Arrange to spend time with these special people. Seek out the company of people who energize you, not those who drain you.

People and activities that give me energy...

....
....
....
....
....
....
....
....
....
....
....
....
....

Surrender to what is.

Let go of what was.

Have faith in what will be.

Sonia Ricotti

is for
Quiet

The classic image of mindfulness is of a monk or yogi sitting cross-legged in a state of peaceful contemplation. And while stillness and silence are not essential for mindfulness, they are certainly valuable.

It is of course possible to be mindful while surrounded by noisy traffic, a turbulent storm or loud drilling. However, finding some degree of stillness and quiet – both metaphorically speaking and in terms of actual noise – can really help, especially when you are new to mindfulness practice.

It is not just about finding a quiet place; it's about not engaging with whichever sounds your mind chooses to focus on. Learning to filter out the sounds that interrupt our focus can be hugely helpful to our stress levels, so our mind is freed from constantly scanning for sounds requiring a mental response.

When we are particularly tired or stressed, we can become hypersensitive to noises. It is an act of generosity to your mind to switch off the radio or music sometimes and sit or lie in peaceful stillness. This is an ideal state for performing a breathing meditation or body scan, which will leave you nurtured and centred. Finding a quiet spot in a natural setting will enhance this sense of stillness and balance.

My daily affirmations:

1. ....
....
....

2. ....
....
....

3. ....
....
....

Quiet the mind and

the soul will speak.

Ma Jaya

is for
Respect

Living a fulfilling life means having a respectful attitude to the world and everything in it – including yourself. Incorporating mindfulness into your daily life means committing to yourself and taking responsibility for your own path.

Learning to say no is also a huge step in gaining control of your life. If you are already feeling overburdened and somebody asks you to do something, it is OK to say no. In fact, it is an act of respect to yourself not to spread yourself too thinly. You wouldn't expect other people to take on too much, so apply those same standards to yourself. In respecting yourself, you will ultimately have more energy to devote to others.

Taking the time and attention to appreciate the little things demonstrates a respect for life and the world. You can do so by trying one of these mindful exercises:

- Observe tiny details, such as a snail making its way across a path, a spider spinning its web or the particular light as the sun first rises in the morning.
- When you are walking along a riverbank, fall into pace with the river, feeling at one with its flow. Pick out a piece of floating debris on the surface and share its journey, matching its speed.
- Find a dry, peaceful spot in a natural setting. Lying on your back, watch the sky changing above you. Shift your focus to noticing your body weight, spread out, sinking into the earth.

Don't worry if you don't get the hang of these exercises straight away. Be patient with yourself.

I can be respectful by...

1. ....
....
....

2. ....
....
....

3. ....
....
....

I can be respected by...

1. ....
....
....

2. ....
....
....

3. ....
....
....

The world is
full of wonder.
I can find meaning
in my life.

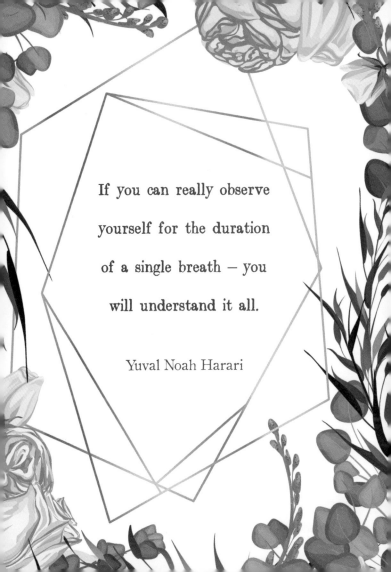

If you can really observe
yourself for the duration
of a single breath — you
will understand it all.

Yuval Noah Harari

is for
Serenity

Mindfulness is not about achieving objectives; it's about acceptance and appreciation of what's around you and in you. With practice, it is possible to achieve emotional calm in the present moment by harnessing the power of your imagination. Imagine a scene where you feel completely at peace – whether it's an imaginary tropical island, a quiet woodland glade or a favourite childhood spot. You can visit this place any time you like in your mind, to achieve an authentic sense of calm. This is known as transcendental meditation.

Close your eyes and imagine your restful place. Make this image as vivid as possible. Really bring it into being with as many sensory details as you can. For example, see the rays of sun slicing through the branches and waves gently rippling on the water's surface, hear a bird's wings whirring against the water, smell the sweet scent of cherry blossom, feel the softness of the bright moss, savour the taste of a fresh fig... any sensation that fits and is personal to your scene. Sink into a deep relaxation and experience a sincere sense of gratitude as you explore your personal oasis. When you are ready to leave, open your eyes and return to the present.

Another essential ingredient for serenity and harmony is quality sleep. Avoid caffeine and other stimulants, and make your bedroom a screen-free sanctuary. Invest in luxury bedding and pillows. Give yourself the opportunity for a full eight hours' sleep whenever you can and enjoy the restorative benefits.

Sketch or write down anything that epitomizes or conveys the concept of "peace" for you.

Allow yourself to be free in your interpretation.

Tune into
the present
moment with
every breath.

T

is for
Thankfulness

Expressing gratitude is fundamental to appreciating what you have rather than focussing on what you might want. Gratitude is associated with increased empathy, mental well-being and happiness, and giving thanks should be heartfelt and sincere.

Learn to accept offers of help with grace and gratitude, rather than automatically saying no and shutting down someone's goodwill. Consider how good it makes you feel when you help another person or animal and when that individual is thankful for your help. Allow others to do that for you.

Being thankful for everything around us is a gentle reminder to experience the world mindfully. If you're caught in a heavy rain shower, instead of worrying about getting wet, marvel in each droplet of rain and water's remarkable power to sustain life.

Gratitude grows the more you feed it, so spend a little time each day cultivating your thankfulness by acknowledging all the wonderful aspects of your life. You can incorporate gratitude into your daily schedule in any way you like. You could recite a personal mantra every morning to embrace that goodwill, or at the end of each day write a note about something you are thankful for on a piece of coloured paper and place it in a glass jar – the jar will become a cheerful visual reminder of all the things you have to be thankful for. You could also instigate a daily ritual with your family at the dinner table, taking it in turns to express thanks for one aspect of your day.

Today I am thankful for...

1. ....
....
....

2. ....
....
....

3. ....
....
....

Peace can't be achieved in the outside world unless we have peace on the inside.

Goldie Hawn

is for
Uplift

What makes you feel uplifted? A walk on the beach, a special meal, a favourite book, a feel-good movie, a night out with friends? Or perhaps a swim, a family picnic, a cuddle with a pet or loved one, a board game or an aromatherapy massage?

Is there anything you used to love doing that you stopped because life got too busy? If so, make time for it again.

Touch is an important and powerfully calming sense that we don't use often enough. Book yourself a relaxing massage, or take turns with a friend giving each other shoulder massages. Taking time to share physical touch is wonderfully therapeutic, and self-massage is also beneficial.

Perhaps indulging in a relaxing bath, with candles around the edge, is all you need to feel centred again.

Another simple trick to uplift your spirits is to tackle a small task rather than putting it off until later. You can then enjoy the satisfaction of ticking it off your to-do list.

Choose a single object, sound or smell and really focus on it. Write down descriptive words to try to capture it.

You can't calm the storm,

so stop trying.

What you can do

is calm yourself.

The storm will pass.

Timber Hawkeye

is for
Visualization

Mindfulness is about engaging with the present moment, but it is of course sometimes necessary to plan or contemplate the future. And, in fact, the mental clarity that mindfulness delivers is precisely what can help us to make good decisions regarding what we want to do with our lives.

Visualizing future events can be enormously effective, as well as comforting, as it gives us something to work toward. People who use visualization techniques and write down their plans are more likely to achieve them. Picturing it, dreaming it and writing it down is a powerful way of committing to it. Effective visualization is subtly different from setting yourself hard goals; its remit is broader.

Instead of trying to achieve everything you want in life now, pick a point a few years from now and imagine how you'd like your life to be. Be realistic; there's no point picturing yourself owning a desert island and a fleet of yachts with a movie star partner. Imagine what would actually give you satisfaction. You might come up with a very simple picture.

How does your visualization compare to what your life looks like right now?

Practising visualization can not only help you improve your focus, it can also lower your stress, improve your performance, enhance your preparedness and give you the extra energy or motivation you might need to accomplish your goals.

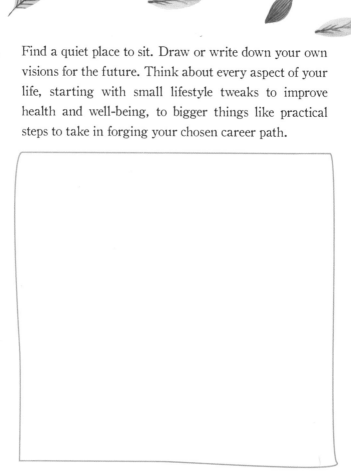

Find a quiet place to sit. Draw or write down your own visions for the future. Think about every aspect of your life, starting with small lifestyle tweaks to improve health and well-being, to bigger things like practical steps to take in forging your chosen career path.

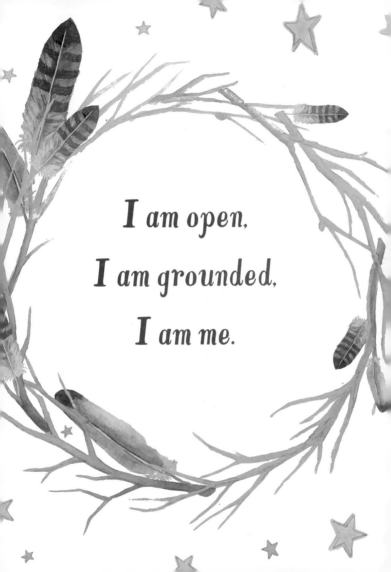

I am open,
I am grounded,
I am me.

is for
Walk

The simple act of walking can become a mindful activity. You can focus on the rhythm of your footsteps, on the sound of your breathing, on the feeling inside your chest. Observe your leg and buttock muscles working and your arms swinging. Notice how your feet connect with the ground. Zone in on sights, sounds and smells. Open your awareness to everything around you.

To enhance this experience, try a sensory walk.

1. Go outside, perhaps to your garden if you have one, or to an area of parkland or woodland. Make sure there is nothing sharp on the ground, then take off your shoes and socks and feel the world through your feet. Observe how much sensory information you are able to take in from your feet alone. How does the surface feel? Is it hard, soft, slippery, gritty? Is it even or uneven, warm or cold? Do you normally notice these things when you are wearing shoes?

2. Observe the light, shade and colours around you. Close your eyes. What do you notice now? Making sure there are no branches or obstacles at head height, take a few steps. Reach out and touch a tree or a wall, or reach down and touch the grass, gravel or paving. How does it feel?

3. Now notice sounds and smells. Do these senses heighten, too? Are you aware of anything you weren't aware of before? For sighted people, sight tends to dominate our senses. Closing your eyes allows your senses of touch, sound and smell to amplify.

Without a conscious plan, pick up a pencil or pen and do a simple squiggle. Then continue the doodle from one end of your line. Let your hand move freely. Finally, join your line up with the starting point of your squiggle, so you have a single, continuous line that you can follow with your finger. Put down your pen and study your doodle. Does anything start to take shape out of it – a dragon, a fish, an eye? Fill in some areas between the lines and see if your squiggle becomes something else. A formless doodle is as valid as anything else; the point is to allow yourself the freedom to make a mark on the page and explore what happens. Avoid judging or criticizing your doodle. Just experience the freedom of creation without any rules or expectations.

Just observe the reality

of the present moment,

whatever it may be.

S. N. Goenka

Release,

restore,

rebalance.

X

is for
X-Ray

Imagine taking a metaphorical X-ray of your life. Nothing is hidden from your X-ray. Is there anything fractured or in need of attention?

You can also imagine an X-ray of your body. Do any problem areas show up? If they do, in a gentle and forgiving way, bring your attention to these areas to give them a little much-needed TLC. Think of it as investing in them. Give them a little extra energy and focus today, and tomorrow they will repay you with interest. You can repeat your X-ray exercise weekly and observe without judgement whether there have been any changes.

Now perform a mental X-ray. How are you doing? Could you do with a bit of self-attention? If so, be generous and mindful, and give yourself that attention your mind is craving! It will appreciate every extra bit of attention you can give it. Accept any thanks your mind wishes to give.

Now, imagine you are wearing X-ray goggles that enable you to see right through things to their core. Use these goggles in different scenarios. For example, you might see right into the goodness in the heart of a friend, or you might see the value in practising something that you want to improve at. Or on a nature walk, you might use your X-ray goggles to see right inside a tree, witnessing the flow of water from roots to leaves. Have fun and be creative with your X-ray powers!

Think of a time when you felt happy and carefree. Take a mental X-ray and describe the memory, including as many specific details as you can.

....
....
....
....
....
....
....
....
....
....
....
....
....

Be patient.

Relax and trust.

Let go.

Then, let go some more.

Melody Beattie

is for
Yoga

With its focus on the breath, body and mind, yoga goes hand in hand with mindfulness. In yoga, the breath is seen as the constant connection to the present moment. When we focus our attention on our breath, we have no choice but to be in the present.

Through a series of postures or *asanas*, individuals move at their own pace, within their own abilities and limitations. Since it is inherently non-competitive and founded on each individual's subjective awareness, anyone can benefit, whether that's at a regular yoga class or in the comfort of home following an audio or video course.

As well as the physical benefits of increased flexibility, strength and muscle tone, deeper breathing, alleviation of chronic pain and protection against injury, many people who practise yoga find it boosts their vitality, mental clarity and overall well-being. Even a simple stretching sequence performed regularly can deliver significant benefits.

Another low-impact option for people of all ages and fitness levels is t'ai chi, a series of gentle, flowing movements founded in Chinese culture. Also known as t'ai chi ch'uan, it combines deep breathing with movement to restore balance and reduce stress.

Design your own mandala below. Try to incorporate some details that mean something to you. You could copy your mandala onto blank card and give it to a friend to colour in, to share the benefits of your mindfulness.

I am at peace
with who I am.

is for
Zoom

Practise widening and narrowing your focus. This is an excellent exercise to help you hone your mental clarity. Imagine you're a camera with a zoom lens. You can zoom in and out on anything you like. Practise zooming in on one of your five senses, and observe, without any evaluation, what is there. Then zoom out and experience all of your senses at once. If you find any aches and pains during your daily body scan or breathing meditation, you can return later with your zoom lens and focus some attention on that specific area.

Use whatever technique works for you. Some people picture a soft blue spot gently moving around their body and settling in areas that need its calming effect. Others like to visualize an energy field concentrated on a specific site. Or imagine a tight coil unwinding, or a soluble disc dissolving the pain, like an effervescent vitamin C tablet placed in the centre of the ache.

You can bring your internal camera to any situation. Use it in a natural setting to focus on minute details – the intricate veining in a leaf, or a particular animal call. Or zoom into particular flavours in a meal – for example, individual spices in a curry. Can you differentiate distinct flavours? You could even use your zoom lens to spice up an otherwise boring meeting. Notice how zooming in and out of any situation alters your perception and field of view. Use it with a sense of freedom and exploration as you advance your mindfulness practice.

Jot down some words to remind you to live in the present moment. As well as more general terms, think of words that are specific to you that could trigger your awareness and focus your attention.

There are deep wellsprings of peace

and contentment living inside us all...

They're just waiting to be liberated.

Mark Williams

You can only live

tomorrow after you

have lived today.

Smile,
breathe and
go slowly.

Thích Nhất Hạnh

Conclusion

I hope you have enjoyed this book. Evaluation and assessment are essential to navigate life. You see a crocodile in the river; you judge it to be dangerous to your life; you make a decision not to cross the river. You see a car approaching. Your brain processes this information, telling you to wait before crossing the road. Every day our lives are full of hundreds of thousands of decisions, some of them conscious, many of them automatic.

And yet if evaluation and appraisal play too active a role in our thoughts, they can be the enemies of a calm and joyful life. A continuous stream of judgements can be stressful and exhausting. Our minds can become overactive and overstimulated. Self-criticisms and admonishments can destroy our confidence and joy.

That's where mindfulness comes in. That's when you need to call in the tamer. But that tamer is you. However much your inner dialogue tries to put you down, guilt-

trip you or tell you what you did was wrong, you can take back control. It will take practice, but it's easy once you've got the knack.

Mindfulness is not just another fad; it's been practised in Eastern traditions for thousands of years. Armed with the tools to use it, you can now embrace mindfulness to transform your own life. I wish you joy and luck in your journey.

Image credits

pp.1, 3–5, 8–9, 14, 26–7, 36, 40, 44, 48, 52, 56–7, 62, 66–7, 72, 84–5, 90, 94, 98, 102, 106, 112, 116, 120, 124–5, 126, 128 – watercolour leaves © Anastasia Panfilova/Shutterstock.com

pp.15, 28, 37, 59, 69, 73, 95, 113, 117 – watercolour backgrounds © Anassia Art/Shutterstock.com

pp.10, 41, 53, 63, 86, 99, 108, 123 – watercolour backgrounds © Rolau Elena/Shutterstock.com

pp.23, 29, 68, 77, 81, 87, 109, 121 – leaves and flowers © Gluiki/Shutterstock.com

p.103 – wreath © Eisfrei/Shutterstock.com

pp.5, 45, 122, 125 – poppies © Anastasia Panfilova/Shutterstock.com

pp.9, 57 – clouds © Nadezhda Eltanets/Shutterstock.com

pp.11, 19, 33, 49, 58, 91, 127 – watercolour leaves and flowers © VerisStudio/Shutterstock.com

p.18 – mandala © Lovely Mandala/Shutterstock.com

p.32 – mandala © Lano4ka/Shutterstock.com

p.62 – mandala © Katika/Shutterstock.com

pp.45, 124 – feather wreath © natika/Shutterstock.com

p.36 – tree-trunk line drawing © pitch-ya/Shutterstock.com

Illustrated letters throughout © VerisStudio/Shutterstock.com

Watercolour spots throughout © Alena Tselesh/Shutterstock.com

If you're interested in finding out more
about our books, find us on Facebook at
Summersdale Publishers and follow
us on Twitter at @**Summersdale.**

www.summersdale.com